MW01602592

Original title:
Eternal Bonds

Author: Lan Donne
ISBN HARDBACK: 978-9916-86-869-0
ISBN PAPERBACK: 978-9916-86-870-6
ISBN EBOOK: 978-9916-86-871-3

The Heart's Map

In whispers soft, the stars align,
They sketch a path, a subtle sign.
With every beat, the world unfolds,
A journey drawn in shades of gold.

Across the hills where shadows play,
Love carves the way, a bright array.
Through valleys deep and rivers wide,
The heart's brave pulse, our faithful guide.

Each twist and turn, a tale is spun,
In every shadow, warmth from sun.
A compass made of dreams and scars,
We chase the light, we reach for stars.

The map unrolled, its ink anew,
With every step, we walk what's true.
Together bound, in laughter's grace,
We find our way, we find our place.

So hold this treasure close and tight,
The heart's own map, our purest light.
Through storms and calm, we'll navigate,
For love's the road that won't abate.

Ageless Ties

In quiet moments, hands entwine,
Echoes linger, your heart in mine.
Through whispered days, we softly tread,
Each memory blooms where love has led.

Time may pass, yet bonds remain,
Life's rich tapestry, woven in grain.
Through seasons' change, we stand side by side,
Ageless ties, in love we abide.

Tides of Togetherness

Like waves that dance upon the shore,
Together we rise, forevermore.
In the ebb and flow, we find our place,
A rhythm of hearts, a gentle embrace.

When storms arise, we hold on tight,
Our spirits soar, through darkest night.
In laughter and tears, our souls align,
Tides of togetherness, yours and mine.

Harmonies of Heartstrings

In softest tunes, our hearts do sing,
A melody sweet, the joy you bring.
With every note, our spirits soar,
Together we dance, forever more.

In sync we move, through thick and thin,
Harmonies played with love within.
A symphony bright, our lives compose,
Heartstrings entwined, as love still grows.

Chronicles of Connection

Pages turned in life's grand book,
Between each line, a loving look.
Stories shared in laughter and tears,
Chronicles written over the years.

In quiet whispers, truths unfold,
Of dreams and hopes, of hearts bold.
Through every chapter, hand in hand,
Connections weave, like fine, soft sand.

Bridges Built from Love

Between the shores we stand tall,
Creating bonds that will not fall.
With every step, our hands entwined,
A future bright, our hearts aligned.

Through storms and trials, we won't sway,
Together we'll find a bright new day.
With every laugh, with every tear,
Our love's a bridge that knows no fear.

Celestial Journeys Together

Underneath the velvet sky,
We chase the stars as they pass by.
Hand in hand, we float like dreams,
In galaxies, we're more than schemes.

With every wish upon the night,
Our love ignites a wondrous flight.
Through nebulas, our spirits soar,
Together we explore much more.

Footprints in the Sand

Along the shore, we walk as one,
With every wave, a day begun.
Our laughter mixes with the breeze,
In footprints that the tide won't seize.

Memories made beneath the sun,
In gentle whispers, our hearts run.
As time flows on, we'll hold this way,
Our bond remains, come what may.

Echoes of Time

In shadows cast by moments past,
We listen close, the echoes last.
Through corridors of dreams we roam,
In every whisper, we find home.

With every tick, the stories weave,
In threads of gold, we choose to believe.
The past and future intertwine,
In echoes, love's sweet design.

Forever Entwined Stories

In whispers of the night, we share,
Tales of joys and endless care.
With every glance, our hearts align,
Two souls as one, in fate we shine.

Through laughter's echo, shadows play,
Every moment, bright as day.
We weave our dreams, with tender threads,
Together in the life we've led.

The Roots of Our Togetherness

Deep in the earth, our roots entwine,
Strengthened by love, through space and time.
With every storm, we stand so tall,
In unity, we'll never fall.

Together we have found our place,
In every heart, we leave a trace.
Bound by the strength of what we share,
Nurtured by love, forever rare.

Through Seasons Unfading

Winter's chill and springtime bloom,
Each season holds a perfect room.
Through autumn leaves and summer's glow,
Our love, a constant, always grows.

In every change, we learn and grow,
With hand in hand, we face the flow.
Time may pass, but hearts remain,
In every sun and every rain.

Remnants of Unyielding Affection

In every glance, the spark ignites,
A bond that's strong, through darkest nights.
Memories linger, sweet and bright,
In the silence, love takes flight.

Through trials faced, we still believe,
In every turn, we shall achieve.
The remnants of our sweet embrace,
Echo in time, a timeless grace.

The Gold of Togetherness

In laughter's embrace, we find our way,
With hearts intertwined, come what may.
Through storms and sunshine, side by side,
Together we stand, our strength our guide.

The moments we share, a treasure to hold,
In whispers of love, our stories unfold.
With hands held tight, the path is bright,
In the gold of togetherness, shines pure light.

Threads of Destiny

In the loom of fate, our lives are spun,
Each thread unique, yet we are one.
With colors vibrant, our dreams take flight,
Bound by the journey, stitched in the night.

The fabric of time we weave with care,
In every strand, a story rare.
Though paths may wander, and distances grow,
The threads of destiny always flow.

Celestial Lights

Across the night sky, the stars gleam bright,
Whispers of wonder in the soft twilight.
Each twinkle tells tales of love and grace,
In the dance of the heavens, we've found our place.

The moon's tender glow, a guiding friend,
In shadows it lingers, on paths we wend.
Together we gaze at the cosmic show,
Under celestial lights, our spirits glow.

Mosaic of Memories

Each piece a moment, bright and true,
In the mosaic we build, me and you.
With laughter and tears, we shape our days,
In colors of time, our story displays.

Fragments of joy, of heartache and dreams,
In the portrait of life, love brightly beams.
Together we craft this beautiful art,
A mosaic of memories, woven from heart.

The Language of Love

In whispers soft and gentle tones,
Hearts converse in sweet unknowns.
Every look a silent plea,
A dance that sets the spirit free.

Through laughter shared and tears that fall,
Words unspoken, they say it all.
In every touch, a promise made,
In moments small, a life displayed.

The warmth of hands, a tender squeeze,
A language spoken in the breeze.
With every heartbeat, love's refrain,
A symphony that eases pain.

In dreams we meet, in stars we trust,
In fleeting moments, hope is a must.
Together weaving skies above,
In every breath, the language of love.

Roots That Nourish

Beneath the soil, where shadows lie,
Roots entwine, they touch the sky.
In silence strong, they hold the ground,
Through storms and drought, their strength is found.

They draw the life from earth's embrace,
With every season, they find their place.
In whispered winds, their tales unfold,
Of ancient lives and dreams retold.

The branches dance, a story spun,
From depths below, the growth begun.
Each leaf a memory, green and bright,
Nourished by the soft moonlight.

Together bound, in harmony,
Roots and branches weave like poetry.
In every storm, they face the strife,
These roots that nourish, give us life.

Flickers of Forever

In candlelight, where shadows play,
Moments spark and drift away.
A glance, a smile, they seem so small,
Yet hold the power to enthrall.

Flickers of joy in fleeting time,
Echoes soft, like distant chime.
Every heartbeat, a wish ignites,
In quiet corners, love's delight.

Through summers bright and winters cold,
These fleeting sparks are stories told.
With every laugh, with every tear,
Life's tapestry, woven year by year.

In memories, we find our spark,
Each flicker brightens up the dark.
Together, we create and weave,
Flickers of forever, we believe.

Symphony of Silences

In hushed whispers, the world unfolds,
A symphony that silence holds.
Notes unplayed, yet understood,
In quiet corners, stillness stood.

Each breath a rhythm, soft and pure,
In the calm, we find our cure.
In every pause, a story waits,
A language rich, that silence creates.

The rustle of leaves, the whispering trees,
Nature's voice carried on the breeze.
A symphony built on hearts that feel,
In silence, truths begin to heal.

So listen close to the quiet songs,
In silence, we discover where we belong.
In every heartbeat, in every sigh,
A symphony of silences, we can't deny.

An Unbroken Path

Step by step, the journey flows,
With every turn, the spirit grows.
In winding trails, we find our way,
Through light and shadow, come what may.

Each footprint left is a story told,
In whispers soft, the brave and bold.
Together we walk, hand in hand,
On this unbroken, golden strand.

Past valleys low and mountains high,
Beneath the vast, embracing sky.
With hope as our guiding star above,
We travel the path, united in love.

The road ahead may twist and bend,
But with our hearts, we will transcend.
Through every challenge, we will soar,
On this unbroken path, forevermore.

So let us march with heads held high,
With faith as wide as the endless sky.
In unity, our spirits clasp,
With every step, we'll tightly grasp.

Love's Infinite Loop

In every glance, a spark ignites,
In whispered words, our dreams take flight.
Around and 'round, the feelings flow,
In love's embrace, we always grow.

Through laughter shared and moments rare,
We intertwine, a perfect pair.
With open hearts, we dive in deep,
In this circle, our souls will keep.

A dance of joy, a waltz of trust,
With every beat, it feels so just.
In the rhythm of morning's light,
Our love loops on, forever bright.

Like tides that rush to kiss the shore,
In love's embrace, we crave for more.
The infinite loop that knows no end,
A sacred bond, forever mend.

Together we weave a vibrant thread,
A tapestry of what's unsaid.
Through every twist, our hearts entwine,
In this infinite loop, you are mine.

Seasons of Connection

In springtime's bloom, our hearts align,
With petals soft, and sun that shines.
New life begins, a dance so sweet,
In nature's cheer, our souls compete.

Summer arrives with warmth's embrace,
In laughter loud, we find our space.
With rays of gold, our spirits soar,
In every moment, we crave more.

As autumn paints with amber hues,
In falling leaves, we share our views.
With crisp air's kiss, we hold so tight,
In every sunset, we find our light.

Then winter spreads its quiet white,
In candle's glow, we find our sight.
In cuddled warmth, we pause and rest,
In frosty breaths, we feel so blessed.

Through changing tides, our bond will last,
In every season, present and past.
Together we face the storms and sun,
In seasons of connection, we are one.

A Universe of Us

In the stardust of the night sky,
Our dreams converge, as planets fly.
With galaxies twinkling, hearts align,
In a universe of love divine.

With every heartbeat, stars will sing,
In cosmic dance, our spirits cling.
Through nebulae and distant light,
We journey on, ever so bright.

A million moments, intertwined,
In this vast space, our hearts confined.
With constellations holding our fate,
In a universe of love, we create.

As comets blaze and meteors fall,
In the silence, we hear love's call.
Through stellar winds, we drift as one,
In this endless sky, our love has spun.

In the cosmos wide, we find our place,
With every spark, we feel the grace.
In the infinite, beneath its trust,
We thrive, together, a universe of us.

The Song of Us

In whispered dreams we twine,
Our hearts beat in the night.
A melody divine,
Two souls in softest light.

Together we shall soar,
Through storms that test our way.
With love, we shall restore,
The dawn that greets the day.

Through laughter and through tears,
We'll share the endless road.
Each moment calms our fears,
Together we are whole.

Let echoes linger near,
In harmony we find,
A song that all can hear,
Two voices intertwined.

With every step we take,
A symphony unfolds.
In memories we make,
A tale that's yet untold.

Beyond the Sands of Time

In whispers of the breeze,
Old memories resound.
We chase the fleeting seas,
Where dreams and hopes are found.

Each grain tells a story,
Of love that once was near.
Through shadows, seeking glory,
In moments we hold dear.

As stars begin to fade,
We ponder what is lost.
With every choice we made,
Our hearts forever crossed.

Beyond the sands we tread,
Lies promise yet to bloom.
In every tear that's shed,
We rise from darkest gloom.

Time weaves its gentle thread,
In patterns soft and bold.
Together, love we've bred,
A tale of hearts of gold.

The Bridge Between Us

A bridge of whispered words,
Linking hearts across the space.
With gentle truths, we've stirred,
A chorus of embrace.

Though rivers may arise,
We hold each other tight.
In storms and sunny skies,
You are my guiding light.

With every step we take,
The distance fades away.
In trust we will awake,
To find a brand new day.

Through laughter and through strife,
This bridge will never break.
Together, we find life,
In every step we make.

So here's to paths unseen,
Where love will always lead.
In moments sweet and keen,
We are each other's need.

Threads of the Past

In shadows softly cast,
The stories weave and blend.
With every thread held fast,
Our journeys never end.

Worn pages filled with grace,
Hold laughter, love, and pain.
In each familiar place,
The echoes still remain.

The tapestry we spin,
Is colored by our dreams.
Through thick and through thin,
We mend the fragile seams.

Though time may fade away,
The threads will hold us tight.
In weaving night and day,
We find our shared light.

Together, side by side,
We honor what has passed.
With love as our guide,
We'll cherish threads that last.

A Song Without End

In whispers soft, the night calls me,
Melodies dance like waves at sea.
Every note, a breath of time,
Echoes linger in a silent rhyme.

Stars align in a cosmic hush,
Dreams awaken, heartbeats rush.
With open eyes, we chase the light,
A song unfurls in the heart of night.

Forever sung, this tune we share,
In every heartbeat, in every prayer.
Time unwinds, yet we remain,
Bound together in love's sweet chain.

Through shadows deep and skies so wide,
In every sorrow, in every tide.
Our laughter sings, a vibrant blend,
Toward horizons where dreams transcend.

So let the years like rivers flow,
In the symphony, we'll always know.
A song without end, a timeless thread,
In the tapestry of life, we're gently wed.

Constellations of Connection

Beneath the vast and starlit dome,
We find our paths, we find our home.
Each star a bond, each light a spark,
Illuminating shadows, brightening dark.

In silence shared, our spirits soar,
Like constellations through endless lore.
Every glance speaks, each touch ignites,
A universe woven in shared delights.

In galaxies distant, our dreams collide,
A cosmic dance, together we glide.
Through the chaos, we find our way,
Hand in hand, come what may.

Connecting hearts through infinite space,
In this journey, we find our place.
Each moment cherished, a shimmering thread,
In constellations of connection, we're led.

So let the stars bear witness tonight,
To the love that glows, so pure, so bright.
In the fabric of time, our stories blend,
A tapestry where the universe bends.

The Weave of Us

Threads of laughter, threads of tears,
In the fabric of life, through the years.
Every moment, a stitch we make,
In the weft and warp, our hearts awake.

Woven together, strong and free,
In a tapestry, just you and me.
Colors blend with every embrace,
A portrait of love, time can't erase.

Through the storms and sunny skies,
In every challenge, our spirits rise.
With hands entwined, we navigate,
In the weave of us, we celebrate.

Each memory crafted, a pattern true,
In this masterpiece, I see you.
Every fragment, each piece aligns,
In the weave of us, our love defines.

So let the world unravel fast,
In our embrace, forever cast.
A tapestry rich, a dance so grand,
In the weave of us, we always stand.

Emblem of the Heart

In the quiet glow of twilight's grace,
Love takes form, a sacred space.
An emblem born from whispers shared,
A testament to the lives we dared.

With every heartbeat, it finds its way,
A compass found in love's ballet.
In this emblem, a story flows,
Of dreams pursued and the faith that grows.

Through trials faced and joys embraced,
In every choice, our love's interlaced.
A symbol bright against all fears,
An emblem crafted from laughter and tears.

So here we stand, hand in hand,
In life's great journey, together we land.
This emblem cherished, a light so bright,
Guiding our souls through the darkest night.

Forever marked by passion's fire,
In the heart's embrace, we find our desire.
An emblem of the heart, beautifully cast,
A love unyielding, meant to last.

The Flame That Never Dimmed

In the dark, a spark ignites,
A beacon shining through the night.
Whispers of hope dance in the air,
A warmth that lingers everywhere.

Through the storms that rage and howl,
It stands its ground, a steady prowl.
A flicker bold, it does not fade,
A promise made, forever laid.

In shadows deep, where dreams reside,
The flame persists; it will not hide.
A radiant glow, a flame so true,
Endless light, forever new.

With every beat, a heart aligns,
Fires of love in endless signs.
Together we stand, hand in hand,
A bond unbroken, forever fanned.

So let the world keep turning round,
In every heart, the flame is found.
Together we rise, forever swim,
In love's embrace, the flame won't dim.

Ink on an Infinite Page

Words flow like rivers, deep and wide,
Stories born with every stride.
Inky thoughts on parchment lie,
Dreams take flight, they soar and fly.

Each letter dances, moves with grace,
A timeless journey through time and space.
Pages turn, a tale unfolds,
Secrets whispered, legends told.

Each mark a heartbeat, pure and free,
A universe spun from you and me.
Ink spills magic, colors our fate,
Writing life's story, never too late.

In silence, we find the gentle sound,
Of scripts entwined, ever profound.
With every pen stroke, possibilities bloom,
In the vast expanse, we carve out room.

Ink on an infinite page, we write,
Of love and dreams, both day and night.
Together, our stories intertwine,
A tapestry rich, forever divine.

Connected by Celestial Threads

Stars twinkle softly from afar,
Each a point, a guiding star.
In the vastness, we find our place,
Connected by light, bound in grace.

Threads of silver weave through the night,
Binding lost souls in cosmic flight.
Celestial whispers, gentle calls,
A tapestry woven, love encompasses all.

In the silence of a midnight sky,
Hearts beat softly as time goes by.
Infinity stretches, holds us near,
In every heartbeat, I sense you here.

Together we traverse the expanse,
Dancing with fate in a timeless dance.
With every pulse, we find our way,
Guided by stars that light our day.

Connected in dreams that twirl and bend,
In this vast universe, we transcend.
Celestial threads pull tight and tight,
In love's embrace, we unite in light.

A Tapestry of Shared Echoes

In the tapestry, stories blend,
Echoes of laughter never end.
Threads of joy, woven with care,
In every stitch, a moment shared.

Colors vibrant, hearts entwined,
Memories flicker, always kind.
Woven together, side by side,
In this fabric, we abide.

Through the threads, our journeys flow,
Tales of love the fibers know.
Secrets stitched with every breath,
In this creation, life and death.

Together we stand in unity,
Fading echoes of serenity.
Hand in hand, we venture forth,
In this tapestry, we find our worth.

With every echo, we are found,
In the silence, love's sweet sound.
A tapestry rich, forever true,
In shared echoes, I find you.

The Tapestry of Us

In colors bright, our stories weave,
Moments shared, we shall not grieve.
Through threads of laughter, love, and tears,
Together we embrace, conquer fears.

Each stitch a memory, radiant glow,
Binding our hearts, in ebb and flow.
Through stormy nights and sunny days,
Our tapestry shines in countless ways.

With every heartbeat, stronger we grow,
In every challenge, together we sow.
The fabric of life, so rich, so vast,
Creating a bond that forever lasts.

In whispers soft, secrets unfold,
In the warmth of embrace, we break the cold.
Every color whispers, soft and clear,
In the tapestry of us, love draws near.

Hand in hand, we travel on,
Woven like a chord in song.
Through winding paths, our spirits soar,
The tapestry of us forevermore.

Heartstrings Across the Divide

In twilight's glow, our spirits sing,
Across the void, love takes wing.
With gentle notes, in silence played,
Heartstrings connect, never to fade.

Distance may stretch, but souls remain,
Tethered by hope, through joy and pain.
In every heartbeat, a whisper true,
Bridges built, just me and you.

When shadows fall and dreams feel far,
Your light, my guide, like a shining star.
In echoes soft of memories shared,
Our heartstrings beat, unprepared.

Through whispered dreams, our voices blend,
In every moment, love transcends.
With every breath across the night,
Heartstrings unite, dispelling fright.

Together we dance, in dreams we weave,
In a symphony where hearts believe.
Across the divide, love shall find,
A timeless bond that's one of a kind.

The Bridge of Time

In the stillness, we stand aligned,
Moments created, soul entwined.
Across the waters, time may flow,
But on this bridge, our love will glow.

With every heartbeat, whispers echo,
In memories held, our spirits grow.
The past, the present, forever one,
Beneath the stars, our journey begun.

Through trials faced and joys embraced,
Each step forward, our lives interlaced.
The tides may change, but we arise,
On the bridge of time, love never dies.

With open arms, we look ahead,
Through every tear, joy shall spread.
In the fabric of fate, we intertwine,
On this bridge of time, your heart is mine.

So let us walk hand in hand, my dear,
Through every season, year by year.
In love we find our steady course,
On the bridge of time, we're joined by force.

Sacred Threads

In sacred threads, our stories spun,
Tales of life, and love begun.
Each weave a promise, each knot a vow,
Together we rise, here and now.

Through laughter shared and tears unspooled,
In threads of faith, our hearts are fueled.
We craft a pattern, rich and rare,
A tapestry woven with utmost care.

With gentle hands, we shape the fate,
In each embrace, we celebrate.
Through trials faced, our bond grows tight,
In sacred threads, we find our light.

In the quiet moments, love does bind,
In every whisper, two souls aligned.
Together we craft dreams anew,
In sacred threads, forever true.

So let love guide us, thread by thread,
In the tapestry of life, joy is spread.
With every heartbeat, our spirits blend,
In sacred threads, on love we depend.

The Bridge Between Us

Two shores that stretch so wide,
Yet every glance, a spark inside.
With whispered dreams, we build a way,
Across the waters, hearts can stay.

In laughter shared and silence sweet,
We find our rhythm, our hearts complete.
Each step we take, a bridge of trust,
In every storm, in love we must.

Through twilight hues and dawn's first light,
We journey forth, with futures bright.
Together standing, hand in hand,
Our bond is strong, like grains of sand.

As footsteps echo on this path,
We write our story, feel the math.
With every stride, our souls align,
In moments brief, our lives entwined.

And when the night brings shadows deep,
In dreams, the promises we keep.
For love's a bridge that won't be tossed,
In time's embrace, we are not lost.

Each Breath a Promise

With every breath, we start anew,
A silent vow, just me and you.
In gentle whispers, hopes ignite,
A promise made beneath the night.

Through trials faced and joys we hold,
These moments precious, stories told.
Each heartbeat echoes, firm and true,
In every sigh, I'm here with you.

The dawn arrives, a canvas bright,
Our dreams adorned with morning light.
In every pause, a chance to see,
The life we weave in harmony.

Through storms that rage and skies that clear,
Your breath, my solace, always near.
With every exhale, love flows free,
A fabric stitched in memory.

And when the shadows seem to close,
We'll stand together, face our foes.
For every breath, a pledge that binds,
In love's embrace, forever finds.

Timeless Moments in Embers

In twilight's glow, the embers gleam,
Holding stories, a whispered dream.
A moment caught within the fire,
Where hearts ignite with pure desire.

Through seasons lost and memories found,
We trace our steps on sacred ground.
Within each spark, a tale unfolds,
A timeless essence, love that holds.

The crackle sings of days gone by,
A dance of shadows, 'neath the sky.
Each flicker tells of joy and pain,
In fleeting warmth, we will remain.

As stars align in velvet skies,
We chase the night, where passion lies.
In starlit whispers, softly spoken,
The bonds of life can't be broken.

So share these moments, let them stay,
Within our hearts, they light the way.
In embers bright, we find our place,
A timeless love that we embrace.

A Symphony of Shared Existence

In chords of life, we find our song,
A melody where we belong.
With notes that dance and rhythms blend,
Our symphony will never end.

Each heartbeat plays a timeless part,
A harmony that stirs the heart.
When joys and sorrows intertwine,
In dissonance, we still align.

Through quiet nights and vibrant days,
We write our lines in varied ways.
With every clash, we find our grace,
A symphony, our saving space.

In gentle echoes, voices rise,
A tapestry beneath the skies.
With every pulse, our spirits soar,
A shared existence, evermore.

Together we compose this tune,
Beneath the sun, beneath the moon.
In every note, forever bind,
A symphony of heart and mind.

Ageless Embrace

In shadows cast by ancient trees,
The whispers of the wind do tease,
Each moment frozen in a dream,
Where love's embrace forever gleams.

The sun dips low, a golden hue,
Soft memories wrapped in morning dew,
With hands held tight, we stand as one,
In timeless space where hearts are spun.

A dance of time, a gentle sway,
Embracing light, we find our way,
Through all the storms that life may bring,
Our love endures, forever sings.

In every glance, a story told,
In every laugh, a joy behold,
Ageless, we wander, hand in hand,
In this vast sea, together we stand.

As seasons change and years unfold,
Our bond remains, a tale of old,
For in each heartbeat, love's refrain,
An ageless tune, forever gain.

Celestial Affection

Beneath the stars, where dreams take flight,
Two souls unite in whispered night,
With every glance, a spark ignites,
In celestial realms, love's purest light.

The moon adorns the velvet sky,
A guardian where our hearts rely,
In constellations, stories weave,
Celestial bonds that never leave.

As comets streak through cosmic seas,
We share a dance, like gentle breeze,
With every heartbeat, love expands,
In endless worlds, we join our hands.

Each twinkle holds a secret dear,
A universe that draws us near,
In silence deep, our wishes soar,
Celestial affection, evermore.

Together we navigate the stars,
Transcending life, beyond our scars,
In this vast space, forever free,
Our love, a timeless galaxy.

The Fabric of Unity

Woven threads of life entwine,
In hues of joy, in shades divine,
We share the fabric, strong and bright,
Unity's strength shines through the night.

With every stitch, our hearts converge,
In harmony, our passions surge,
Together, hand in hand we stand,
Creating peace across the land.

Each tale we tell, a thread anew,
In laughter's joy, in sorrows' hue,
We mend the seams of our design,
The fabric of unity, intertwine.

Through trials faced, we find our way,
In every night, the light of day,
Connected souls, forever bound,
In every heartbeat, love is found.

As colors blend, we rise as one,
In every battle, together won,
A tapestry woven, hearts imply,
The fabric of unity, we rely.

Timeless Intertwining

Waves of time, they ebb and flow,
In moments shared, love tends to grow,
With every glance, a bridge we build,
Timeless paths that fate has filled.

In laughter's echo, memories form,
Through gentle storms, our hearts stay warm,
The roots of trust entwine so tight,
In every shadow, we find light.

As seasons change, we stand our ground,
In every heartbeat, love is found,
Two souls together, fate's sweet line,
In this dance, a spark divine.

A tapestry of dreams we weave,
In every sigh, we learn to believe,
Timeless intertwining, fates align,
In love's embrace, our hearts combine.

With every step, our stories blend,
A journey shared, where heartaches mend,
In this eternal, sacred space,
Timeless intertwining, love's embrace.

Heartstrings in Harmony

In the quiet of the night,
Whispers float on silver beams,
Notes entwine, a sweet delight,
Binding hearts with woven dreams.

Softly strung, the chords align,
Each pulse echoing in time,
Melodies in sweet design,
Gently crafting our shared rhyme.

Through the storm, the music flows,
Guiding us through darkest hours,
As the river of love grows,
Bringing forth the blooming flowers.

With every laugh and every tear,
The symphony of life plays on,
In the rhythm, we draw near,
Together, we forever bond.

So let our heartstrings intertwine,
Creating magic from small sparks,
In harmony, our spirits shine,
Illuminating love's bright marks.

The Dance of Enduring Spirits

Underneath the starry skies,
Spirits twirl in endless grace,
With each step, their love replies,
Echoing time in this space.

Gently swaying in the night,
Their shadows weave a tender tale,
In the moon's soft, silver light,
Together, they shall never pale.

Through the ages, hand in hand,
They embrace both joy and pain,
In the dance, they understand,
Life's sweet music, loss, and gain.

While the world around them fades,
In this moment, they are whole,
A timeless dance serenades,
Filling hearts and warming souls.

As the dawn begins to break,
And shadows stretch toward the light,
Enduring spirits wake and take,
Their love into the morning bright.

Always Returning Home

The open road calls out my name,
With every turn, I trace my past,
In every heartbeat, love's a flame,
Home is where my soul can rest.

Through forest trails and mountain peaks,
Every journey shapes my core,
In silence where my spirit seeks,
I find the place that I adore.

With every sunset's golden glow,
Memories dance within my mind,
The laughter shared, the tears that flow,
In this embrace, my heart is blind.

No matter how far I may roam,
Each winding path leads me right back,
To where the heart knows it's home,
In familiar warmth, I feel no lack.

So let the stars and dreams align,
Guiding me through night's soft dome,
For in the end, the love will shine,
Always leading me back home.

Shadows in Unison

Beneath the weight of twilight's hue,
Shadows stretch and softly sway,
In each silhouette, a truth,
Life's reflections dance and play.

They whisper secrets in the dark,
Unseen yet deeply intertwined,
Every flicker, every spark,
A harmony both sweet and blind.

As the world begins to rest,
Their melody unfolds with ease,
In their presence, I feel blessed,
Lost in time, like autumn leaves.

Together through the night, they glide,
Echoes of a forgotten dream,
In silence, we find our stride,
And savor life's sweet, gentle stream.

Shadows cast by vibrant light,
Remind us we are not alone,
In our hearts, they guide our flight,
Together, we are darkness sewn.

The Symphony of Us

In the quiet night we sway,
Rhythms of hearts in play,
Soft whispers of a tune,
Under the watchful moon.

Every note, a story shared,
Moments lost, moments bared,
Hand in hand, we compose,
A world where love still grows.

With each laugh, we ignite,
A melody of pure light,
Together we rise and fall,
In this symphony, we call.

Through every storm, we stand,
A duet, perfectly planned,
In the silence, we shall trust,
In our music, we adjust.

So let the music play on,
As dawn greets the dawn,
In our hearts, the beat remains,
The symphony forever gains.

Bonds Without Borders

Across the seas and skies,
Our spirits intertwine,
No distance can erase,
The love that knows no line.

Through valleys deep and wide,
Our hearts will find a way,
In laughter or in tears,
Together, come what may.

In every shared embrace,
We bridge the gaps we find,
Joining hands across the miles,
With hope, forever blind.

From cities far and near,
Our stories intertwine,
A tapestry of dreams,
In love, we shall define.

So here we stand as one,
A bond that will not break,
Through time and space we thrive,
For our love's eternal sake.

Memories Etched in Starlight

Underneath the cosmic glow,
We chased the dreams we knew,
Each moment, a piece of time,
In the evening's gentle hue.

With laughter that sparkles bright,
We danced 'neath the velvet sky,
In the glow of distant suns,
Our spirits soared, oh so high.

Pictures formed in vivid threads,
Etched deep upon our souls,
In the canvas of the night,
Our memories make us whole.

Through fleeting cosmic light,
We write our tale in flight,
A journey etched in stardust,
As we drift through dusty night.

So here's to nights divine,
Where our hearts learned to shine,
In the starlit tapestry,
Forever you will be mine.

The Dance of Forever

In the twilight's sweet embrace,
We dance to timeless grace,
Every heartbeat, a step near,
In a rhythm that feels clear.

With every twirl, we share a dream,
As the world fades, we beam,
Lost in the gaze of love's light,
Together we dance, so right.

Round and round, we find our way,
In a waltz that will not sway,
As the stars align up high,
We float beneath the velvet sky.

No end to this sweet embrace,
In the warmth of your space,
Through the whisper of the night,
We dance with pure delight.

So take my hand once more,
Let's spin and never bore,
In this dance of forever,
Our hearts, a splendid tether.

Together in the Realm of Dreams

In a world where shadows play,
We roam beneath the stars' sway.
Colors blend, a cosmic stream,
We find solace in our dream.

Whispers echo, soft and clear,
Together, we have nothing to fear.
Boundless skies, vast and bright,
Holding hands in the quiet night.

Floating on clouds, spirits free,
In this realm, just you and me.
Laughter dances on the breeze,
With every moment, we find ease.

Time drifts softly like a sigh,
In your gaze, I feel I fly.
Dreams intertwine, a woven thread,
In this place, our hearts are led.

With every heartbeat, we create,
A tapestry of love, so great.
Between the stars, we make our mark,
Together in the endless dark.

The Heart's Unfading Map

In the silence, truths unfold,
An ancient tale that must be told.
Each beat draws paths, so divine,
A journey marked with love's design.

Through valleys deep and mountains high,
Our hearts converse, they never lie.
In secret whispers, dreams collide,
In every choice, we turn the tide.

The compass set, our guide is clear,
Navigating through all fear.
With every step, we find our way,
The heart's map leads us, come what may.

In laughter shared and tears we shed,
The paths we've walked, they thread ahead.
Through tempest storms, hand in hand,
With faith, we forge a timeless band.

Each line inscribed, a memory,
Of moments lost, of sweet decree.
Unfading love, our guiding star,
With every heartbeat, near or far.

Celestial Ties of Affection

Stars align in endless night,
Creating bonds with purest light.
In the cosmos, we intertwine,
A love so vast, it's truly divine.

Galaxies swirl, painting the skies,
In your embrace, my spirit flies.
Every twinkle, a promise made,
In the silence, our hearts haven't swayed.

Through constellations, we explore,
Each moment whispers, 'I want more.'
Timeless joy, in cosmic dance,
In your presence, I find my chance.

Drifting softly, like a feather,
Our souls connect, now and forever.
Celestial paths, a wondrous sight,
Together we create our light.

With every pulse, the universe spins,
In this bond, true love begins.
Among the stars, we'll find our place,
In the forever of your embrace.

Threads of Infinity

In the fabric of each day,
Threads of time weave their way.
Moments stitched with love and care,
An endless tapestry we share.

Golden strands of joy and pain,
Each one whispers our refrain.
Through life's loom, we are entwined,
Two souls in fate's design.

With every challenge, every cheer,
Threads of infinity draw us near.
Interwoven hearts, a sacred art,
Bound together, never apart.

In the quiet, in the roar,
Our connection opens every door.
Through the storms and calm we glide,
In unity, we take our stride.

Patterns form in every quest,
Threads of fate, we are blessed.
In this journey, hand in hand,
Together we forever stand.

As the universe spins and twirls,
Each thread reflects our world.
With love as our guiding light,
We weave our dreams in endless night.

Whispers Beyond Time

In shadows cast by distant stars,
Soft voices drift on twilight air.
Memories woven through the years,
Echoes linger, tales laid bare.

A gentle breeze through ancient trees,
Carries secrets, wisdom's grace.
With every sigh, the past concedes,
Yet holds us close in warm embrace.

The nightingale sings to the moon,
Her melody, a timeless spell.
As footsteps fade, we find our tune,
In whispered dreams, we weave so well.

Time dances lightly on our skin,
A fleeting glance, a knowing smile.
Though ages shift, our hearts begin,
To bridge the gaps, to span the miles.

In twilight's grasp, we find our home,
Where moments blend, and silence speaks.
In whispers soft, our spirits roam,
Forever bound, though time's less sleek.

Lifelines of the Heart

Threads of gold entwined in fate,
Each heartbeat a soft refrain.
Through storms and whispers, we create,
A tapestry of joy and pain.

In gentle hands, we hold the light,
Embracing warmth in shadows cast.
With every love, we soar to flight,
A lifeline forged, our bond steadfast.

Through trials faced and laughter shared,
The heartbeats sync in perfect time.
In every glance, the truth declared,
Together we ascend, we climb.

In silence deep, our secrets bloom,
The kindred souls that understand.
In every room, love lifts the gloom,
A lifeline forged, a steady hand.

As seasons change, our spirits grow,
In every heartbeat, trust will weave.
Through ebb and flow, we cherish slow,
The lifelines of the heart we cleave.

Unfading Connections

In the garden where memories grow,
Roots intertwine, seeds of the past.
With every breeze, their tales will flow,
Connections bloom, enduring, vast.

Time may fade the colors bright,
But bonds of love stay evergreen.
In the soft glow of shared twilight,
Together we are always seen.

Through laughter shared and tears that fall,
We navigate this winding road.
In silence deep, we hear the call,
Unfading connections, our abode.

With every chapter, new and old,
The stories echo, never done.
In every heart, a flame to hold,
Unfading love, forever won.

So let the winds of change draw near,
Our spirits blaze through every storm.
In whispers soft, we cast our cheer,
Unfading connections, love's warm form.

Ties That Transcend

Beneath the stars, our spirits soar,
Bound by dreams, forever entwined.
Through every trial, we seek to explore,
The ties that time could never bind.

In moments shared, we find our way,
Across the depths of space and time.
In whispered hopes, we chose to stay,
Each heartbeat known, a sacred rhyme.

Together, through the ebb and flow,
Our laughter dances like the tide.
Wherever life takes us, we know,
The ties that transcend, our hearts abide.

In twilight's glow, our shadows merge,
With every pulse, a bond reaffirmed.
Through life's great symphony, we surge,
In every note, our souls absorbed.

A tapestry of love we weave,
In colors bright and shades profound.
With every breath, we choose to believe,
The ties that transcend forever bound.

Beyond the Veil of Time

Whispers of shadows in the night,
Carried by echoes from days so bright.
Memories linger, though they may fade,
In the heart's chambers, dreams are laid.

Time flows like a river, deep and wide,
In its currents, our secrets abide.
Each tick a promise, each tock a sigh,
Beyond the veil, we soar and fly.

Fleeting moments that shimmer and glow,
Captured in starlight, forever to flow.
Through ages past and futures unknown,
In the dance of time, we are not alone.

A gentle touch, a fleeting glance,
In the realms of time, we take a chance.
For every heartbeat, a tale unfolds,
Beyond the veil, our spirits behold.

Together we wander, hand in hand,
Through the fabric of time, on shifting sand.
United in love, we're never apart,
In the echoes of time, you hold my heart.

The Lingering Dance of Souls

In the quiet hours, spirits entwine,
A dance of shadows, a love divine.
Through whispers soft in twilight's glow,
The lingering dance, a tale we know.

With every heartbeat, a rhythm found,
In the silence, our souls abound.
Waltzing through dreams, we chase the light,
In the embrace of the starry night.

When moments linger, time stands still,
Together we weave, with passion and will.
Through trials faced and laughter shared,
In the dance of souls, we are ensnared.

Though worlds may part and shadows fall,
Our spirits soar, heeding the call.
With every step, we echo the past,
In this timeless waltz, our love shall last.

In the lingering dance, we find our truth,
Eternal flames ignite our youth.
Bound by the cosmos, we journey on,
In the dance of souls, we've just begun.

Resonance of Unspoken Letters

Ink upon paper, words left unsaid,
In the silence, our feelings bled.
Each stroke a whisper, a secret shared,
In unspoken letters, hearts are bared.

Beneath the surface, emotions hide,
In the quiet corners where hopes abide.
Each longing glance, a message clear,
In the resonance, we hold each dear.

Letters linger like shadows at dawn,
In dreams we speak, though the light is gone.
Fragments of thoughts drift through the air,
In unspoken letters, we lay bare.

Memories linger, like scents of the past,
In every heartbeat, our truths amassed.
Words unspoken, yet deeply felt,
In the resonance, our fates have knelt.

So let the silence weave its thread,
In the tapestry of all we've said.
For in the echoes of hearts' endeavor,
In unspoken letters, we are forever.

Endless Tides of Togetherness

Waves of moments crash on the shore,
In the sea of life, we yearn for more.
Tides of laughter, whispers of grace,
In the endless dance, we find our place.

With every sunset, colors collide,
In the embrace of love, we confide.
Through storms and calm, we brave the weather,
In the endless tides, we're bound together.

Footprints in sand, hand in hand,
As we journey through this vast land.
Ebbing and flowing, hearts align,
In endless tides, your soul meets mine.

Seasons change, yet we remain,
In the rhythm of life, joy and pain.
In every heartbeat, a promise true,
In endless tides, I stand with you.

Across the horizon, where dreams reside,
In the waves of love, we take the ride.
Together we wander, forever free,
In the endless tides, just you and me.

Chains of Affection

In soft whispers, hearts entwine,
Promises spoken, yours and mine.
Through trials faced, we stand so strong,
Together, we will prove them wrong.

Bound by memories, laughter shared,
In this journey, love declared.
Through storms and sunshine, side by side,
In our bonds, we will abide.

Time may test, but we won't break,
In each other, we see our fate.
With every glance, a silent vow,
In chains of affection, here and now.

As seasons shift, our roots run deep,
In dreams we chase, the love we keep.
With every heartbeat, close yet free,
In this union, just you and me.

Through the years, our hearts will dance,
In every glance, a second chance.
Together we'll weave a story bright,
In chains of affection, pure delight.

Interwoven Souls

In twilight's grace, two shadows blend,
Silent whispers, the heart's best friend.
In every heartbeat, a tale unfolds,
Interwoven souls, a treasure to hold.

Paths once lonely now intertwined,
In gentle moments, together we find.
With hands held tight, we face the fight,
In harmony's tune, we take flight.

Through winding roads, we journey far,
Guided by love, a shining star.
In every challenge, we grow and learn,
Interwoven souls, forever we yearn.

With every sunrise, hope reborn,
In each other's eyes, we find our dawn.
Through laughter's song and sorrow's toll,
In this dance of life, we are whole.

As seasons change, our roots will stay,
In the depths of love, we'll never stray.
With every heartbeat, a promise true,
Interwoven souls, just me and you.

The Echo of Togetherness

In laughter's echo, our spirits soar,
In gentle silence, we need no more.
Through every sorrow, we find our way,
The echo of togetherness guides today.

In dreams we share, our hopes take flight,
In every glance, a spark ignites.
Through the shadows, our voices blend,
In unity's arms, love knows no end.

With every heartbeat, a rhythm dear,
In the distance, I'll always hear.
The whisper of trust, our bond so true,
The echo of togetherness shines through.

Through darkened nights and brighter days,
In every challenge, our love displays.
Together we stand, come what may,
The echo of togetherness leads the way.

Time may fade, but love remains,
In each memory, joy sustains.
Forever bound, in heart and mind,
The echo of togetherness, sweetly defined.

Enduring Shadows

In the twilight where whispers abide,
Our love lingers, like the evening tide.
Through trials faced, hand in hand,
Enduring shadows, together we stand.

When daylight fades, and doubts arise,
In each other, we'll find the skies.
Through the darkness, love will glow,
Enduring shadows, a steady flow.

With every heartbeat, the past may sway,
But in our arms, the light will stay.
Through the echoes of the night so deep,
Enduring shadows, our promises keep.

Beneath the stars, our dreams take flight,
In the soft glow, we'll chase the night.
With courage born from love's embrace,
Enduring shadows find their place.

As dawn approaches, we'll greet the day,
In every moment, we'll find our way.
Together we'll face whatever falls,
Enduring shadows, love conquer all.

Embracing the Infinite

In the quiet night, stars unfold,
Whispers of dreams, stories untold.
Waves of the cosmos, vast and bright,
We dance with shadows, in eternal light.

Every heartbeat sings a timeless tune,
Between the silence, beneath the moon.
Echoes of laughter, secrets we share,
In a universe wide, we find our care.

Hands intertwined, a celestial chase,
Finding our rhythm, in endless space.
Moments like grains, on the shore they flow,
Embracing the infinite, we come to know.

Through the depths of night, our spirits soar,
Exploring the unseen, forevermore.
With every heartbeat, our souls combine,
In the vastness, our love will shine.

A Journey Without End

Footsteps upon the winding way,
Every dawn brings a brand new day.
With every mile, our hearts expand,
Together we walk, hand in hand.

Mountains high and rivers wide,
We face the storms, stand side by side.
Through valleys deep, where shadows play,
We find the light, come what may.

Every horizon calls us near,
A journey without end, clear and dear.
The road may twist, the path may bend,
With faith in each other, we will transcend.

In fleeting moments, joys unknown,
Glimmers of hope, steadily grown.
Through laughter and tears, our spirits mend,
Embracing the journey, love to send.

Reflections of Us

In mirrors of time, we softly gaze,
Capturing life in a delicate haze.
Every smile shared, a vibrant hue,
Reflections of all that we've been through.

Seasons shift as we turn the page,
Stories written by hearts at age.
With each whisper, the past will sing,
In reflections of us, memories cling.

Through the tempest, through the calm,
Each moment's a thread in our shared psalm.
Colors entwine in a tapestry spun,
Reflections of us, two as one.

With love as our guide, we find our way,
In the garden of life, where shadows play.
A bond so deep, it will never rust,
In every reflection, I cherish us.

The Light in Your Eyes

In twilight's glow, our spirits dance,
There's magic woven in a glance.
The world fades away, the noise subsides,
I see forever in the light in your eyes.

Wonders unravel, secrets unfold,
Stories of warmth and love retold.
With every sparkle, a promise lies,
Illuminating dreams in the light in your eyes.

Through storms we wander, hand in hand,
With faith and hope, together we stand.
In shadows cast, our fervor flies,
Finding solace in the light in your eyes.

Each moment treasured, like waves on shore,
In your gaze, I find the evermore.
A universe wrapped in distant skies,
All I need is the light in your eyes.

Affinity Through the Ages

Through whispers of time, we dance in the light,
In echoes of laughter, our spirits take flight.
The tapestry woven, both delicate and bold,
Threads of our stories, in each heart, unfold.

In shadows we linger, our hands softly meet,
With secrets and dreams, in rhythm, we greet.
Across worlds we wander, in silence, we know,
A bond that transcends, in the ebb and the flow.

With seasons that change, our hearts stay entwined,
In the canvas of life, true colors we find.
Through trials and triumphs, our essence aligns,
An affinity that through all ages defines.

In laughter, in sorrow, together we stand,
With hope as our guide, we create, hand in hand.
Timeless and steadfast, like stars in the night,
Our souls are illuminated, forever in flight.

Through the echoes of past, we journey anew,
In the depth of connection, the universe grew.
For love knows no borders, its waves ever roll,
In the tapestry woven, we each play a role.

The Lighthouses of Our Paths

In the distance, they shine, beacons of our dreams,
Guiding us gently through life's winding streams.
When storms clash around us, their glow holds us true,
Our lighthouses stand firm, in shadows, they grew.

Each light a reminder, we're never alone,
Through fog and despair, their warmth we've known.
With hearts as our compass, we reach for the skies,
Navigating the darkness, where hope never dies.

As waves crash and roar, we find our own way,
With trust in our journey, come night or come day.
With the lighthouses guiding, we dance through the night,

Illuminated paths, in the softest of light.

Their presence a comfort, in moments we falter,
Fueling our spirits, our passion, they altar.
In the whispers of wind, through horizons they gleam,
The lighthouses of life, are the homes of our dream.

Through the ages they stand, unwavering and wise,
Reminders of love's power, in the vastness of skies.
As we sail through the waves, their light will abide,
In the story of us, they're forever our guide.

A Canvas of Memories

In every brushstroke of days gone by,
Shadows of laughter, a soft whispered sigh.
Colorful moments, like petals in bloom,
A canvas of memories, dispelling all gloom.

With sunsets of orange and dawns kissed by gold,
Each picture a story, in each heart, retold.
Where laughter and heartache paint deep on the frame,
A testament of love, timeless and untamed.

The delicate hues of our journey entwined,
Capture the essence of moments defined.
With every regret, a lesson instilled,
In the tapestry woven, our lives are fulfilled.

With family and friends, our colors collide,
In bonds of affection, where joy does reside.
Through the seasons of life, new shades we embrace,
Crafting a masterpiece time cannot erase.

In the gallery of souls, we'll always remain,
In shadows and light, we find joy in the pain.
For every memory cherished, a reminder to see,
The art that we create is our legacy free.

Twin Flames

In the dance of the night, our spirits ignite,
Two flames intertwined, burn fierce and bright.
With each pulse of passion, a rhythm we feel,
Our love an inferno, eternally real.

Through trials and storms, we weather the strife,
In shadows and light, we embrace this life.
Every glance ignites, like kindling anew,
Creating a fire, in all that we do.

With whispers of promise, our hearts align,
In the tapestry woven, your soul calls to mine.
No distance can dim what fate has proclaimed,
The union of spirits, forever unclaimed.

Through echoes of laughter, we rise and we fall,
With strength in our love, we conquer them all.
Together we travel this mystical road,
Two flames in the night, where our passion's bestowed.

In the depths of the night, our light will endure,
With every heartbeat, our bond is secure.
For in this lifetime, our souls will reclaim,
The beauty of love, in the dance of the flame.

Connected Across Worlds

In whispers shared across the void,
Our hearts unite, a bond deployed.
Through distant stars, our dreams will soar,
In every heartbeat, I feel you more.

We navigate these cosmic threads,
In silent language, love's words spread.
The universe, a canvas wide,
On which our hopes and joys abide.

Though miles apart, we're never lone,
In every smile, in every tone.
With every thought, we walk as one,
Connected through the rising sun.

So hold my hand in realms unknown,
Together, we have always grown.
An endless dance, a timeless flow,
In love, the seeds of faith we sow.

As worlds may shift and shadows play,
Our bond will light the darkest day.
Through every struggle, every tear,
In hearts we meet, forever near.

Reflections in Time

Time flows like a gentle stream,
Each moment holds a secret dream.
The past whispers through the years,
In echoes soft, it calms our fears.

Memories dance, a fleeting grace,
In every line, a lover's trace.
We find ourselves in moments brief,
In tender smiles, in shared belief.

Hours blend like colors bright,
Shaping shadows into light.
With every tick, the heart can find,
The beauty of the ties that bind.

So let us pause and drink it in,
In every loss, there's room to win.
Reflections shimmer on the waves,
In time, our love forever saves.

From yesterday, today can rise,
A tapestry beneath the skies.
In every heartbeat, truths unfold,
The stories of our lives retold.

The Garden of Togetherness

In a garden where wildflowers bloom,
Each petal whispers of dreams consumed.
Side by side, hand in hand,
We cultivate a vibrant land.

With laughter shared, we sow our seeds,
In harmony fulfilling needs.
The roots entwined, so deeply bound,
Can weather storms when love is found.

In golden sunlight, we find our peace,
Our hopes and worries drift and cease.
With fragrant blooms, the colors blend,
A tapestry that has no end.

As seasons change, we grow anew,
Together faced with morning dew.
In every challenge, hand in hand,
We cultivate this verdant land.

For in this space, we truly thrive,
In love's embrace, we feel alive.
The garden thrives, forever bright,
A sanctuary of pure delight.

Stars Aligned in Affection

When stars align, our fates entwine,
A cosmic dance, a love divine.
With every glance, the universe sings,
Of whispered dreams and hopeful things.

In starlit skies, our spirits bond,
In midnight hours, we feel so fond.
With every twinkle, soft and bright,
Hope glimmers in the heart of night.

Through endless space, our hearts will roam,
In distant realms, we find our home.
With every heartbeat, the stars conspire,
To light our path with endless fire.

Together we'll soar on wings of love,
Guided by stars in skies above.
With hands held tight against the dark,
In this vast universe, you are my spark.

No boundaries here, just cosmic grace,
In your embrace, I find my place.
As galaxies spin and dreams take flight,
Our love shines brightly in the night.

Rivers of Resonance

Beneath the willow's shade, they flow,
Whispers of memories, soft and low.
Carving paths through stone and time,
Songs of the ages, rhythm and rhyme.

Echoes of laughter dance on the breeze,
Filling the air with gentle ease.
Winding through valleys, they shimmer and glide,
Embracing the earth, a tranquil tide.

Moonlit reflections on the water's face,
A mirror of dreams in this sacred place.
Each ripple tells tales of love and strife,
In the rivers of resonance, we find our life.

Secrets are carried, both old and new,
Stories of hearts that once beat true.
In currents of hope, we journey along,
To the music of nature, our spirits belong.

Flowing forever, their essence imbued,
In each gentle curve, a world renewed.
Rivers of resonance, vast and profound,
In their melody, our souls are unbound.

Echoes of the Heart

In the silence, soft whispers arise,
Fleeting shadows beneath twilight skies.
The heart knows secrets it yearns to share,
Echoes of love linger in the air.

Through moments of laughter and sorrow's embrace,
Each heartbeat whispers a timeless grace.
A symphony plays in the deepest of night,
Illuminating dreams with tender light.

Fragments of joy paint the canvas bright,
In the echoes of the heart, life takes flight.
Memories woven in threads of gold,
Stories of passion and dreams retold.

With every beat, a story unfolds,
The language of love, both tender and bold.
In the quietest moments, we find our way,
Guided by echoes that never betray.

Through valleys of doubt and mountains of fears,
Resilience blooms through the laughter and tears.
In the dance of our hearts, we eternally find,
Echoes of love that forever bind.

Pillars of Light

In the dawn's embrace, they stand so tall,
Pillars of light, answering the call.
Guiding the way through shadows and night,
Illuminating paths, a mesmerizing sight.

With wisdom etched in their ancient forms,
Each beam a promise, as the universe warms.
Resilience flows through their radiant core,
In moments of darkness, they shine evermore.

Beneath their watch, the world comes alive,
Inspiring courage, teaching us to thrive.
Their glow ignites the heart's hidden dream,
A tapestry woven from hope's endless seam.

Through storms and trials, they bear the weight,
Pillars of light never hesitate.
Each flicker a testament, a beacon of grace,
Illuminating love in this vast, boundless space.

In gatherings of souls, they softly shine,
Unraveling fears, entwined and divine.
With every heartbeat, let their essence ignite,
Together we rise, with pillars of light.

Guardians of the Heart

In the stillness, they watch and wait,
Guardians of the heart, love's gentle fate.
With open arms and steadfast grace,
They guide us through life's intricate maze.

Through trials faced and storms we brave,
Their presence holds us, a promise to save.
In whispers of comfort, they'll always stand,
Guardians of dreams, a steadfast hand.

Each heartbeat echoes their unwavering call,
In shadows of doubt, they won't let us fall.
Together they gather, a circle so tight,
Filling the void with luminous light.

Through laughter and tears, they walk by our side,
Guardians of the heart, our eternal guide.
In moments of doubt, they nurture our flame,
In their love's embrace, we're never the same.

With unwavering strength, they shelter our soul,
Encouraging our spirits to always be whole.
Guardians of the heart, timeless and true,
In their boundless love, we continually renew.

Whispers Across Time

In the stillness of the night,
Words drift softly like a breeze,
Carrying tales of old,
Whispers that dance with ease.

Memories spin in twilight's glow,
Echoes of laughter, sweet and light,
Footsteps tracing paths we know,
In dreams that take us to flight.

Gentle murmurs bridge the years,
A tapestry of love and pain,
Through the laughter and the tears,
In every loss, something to gain.

Stars align in endless skies,
As we reach out for the past,
Bound by time, yet free to rise,
Our whispers will ever last.

In the silence, hearts unite,
Across the space of time and tide,
As day turns into night,
In these whispers, we confide.

Threads of Unbreakable Hearts

Two souls woven in the night,
Threads of gold and silver glow,
Stitched with dreams that feel so right,
In this tapestry we sow.

Every laugh, a little thread,
Binding us in joy and care,
In the moments that we've led,
In the love we gladly share.

Through the storms and quiet days,
The fabric of our lives entwined,
In the sun, in shadows' haze,
Together, we are defined.

Every tear, a stitch so strong,
Every moment, colored bright,
In this bond, we both belong,
Unbreakable with all our might.

As we harvest what we've sown,
Fruits of friendship, love's embrace,
With every thread, we've brightly grown,
In our hearts, a sacred space.

The Ties That Bind

Under the vast and starry skies,
Connections form in subtle ways,
Invisible threads that never die,
Binding us through nights and days.

Through laughter, silence, joy, and pain,
We navigate this dance of fate,
In sunshine bright or pouring rain,
These ties grow strong, never late.

In every story shared and told,
In every secret whispered near,
The ties that bind, a gentle hold,
A love that conquers doubt and fear.

With every step, we journey forth,
Hand in hand, the path unwinds,
In every heartbeat, warmth and worth,
In every moment, love reminds.

Together in this life we weave,
A fabric rich with colors bright,
With faith and hope, we still believe,
The ties that bind us shine with light.

Infinite Echoes of Us

In the stillness, echoes rise,
Whispers of the love we know,
Reflections caught in timeless skies,
Through every shadow, we still glow.

With every heartbeat, echoes dance,
A melody that fills the air,
In every glance, a fleeting chance,
To hold the moments we both share.

Across the years, we find our song,
With notes that stretch beyond the day,
In this symphony, we belong,
Resonating in every way.

Memories swirl, a ceaseless tide,
Each wave a story not forgot,
In every breath, we're unified,
Through all the battles that we fought.

As time flows on, our hearts will sing,
Infinite echoes, soft and true,
In every ending, there's a spring,
A timeless dance, just me and you.

The Journey Without an End

Steps whisper on the winding way,
Footprints fade but dreams still stay.
Each horizon calls, we chase the light,
In shadows cast, we find our might.

Through valleys deep and mountains high,
We dance beneath the endless sky.
With every breath, the world unfolds,
A tale of courage yet untold.

Winds may shift and storms may roar,
But hearts united seek the shore.
With laughter shared and tears bestowed,
Together we will bear the load.

The map we draw is ours alone,
With every twist, our courage grown.
Each bend, a challenge to transcend,
Onward we go, the journey's bend.

With every step, we break the norm,
In unity, we weather the storm.
A voyage spun with threads of gold,
In tales of wonder yet unrolled.

Bonds of Starlit Promises

Underneath the velvet sky,
Whispers of the stars float by.
Promises made in glimmered light,
Hearts entwined in cosmic flight.

Each twinkling star a wish we share,
A silent pact, a bond so rare.
Hands clasped tight, we dream aloud,
Lost in wonder, heartbeats proud.

In the night, our secrets dwell,
In stories told, a magic spell.
Boundless dreams from truths we weave,
In starlit skies, we still believe.

The universe sings to us so clear,
Guiding us through love and fear.
With every gaze, our spirits rise,
A tapestry of endless skies.

With every dawn, we find our way,
The bonds we forge will never sway.
Amidst the stars, forever near,
In every heartbeat, you are here.

Portraits of Us Across Millennia

Time-painted faces, echoes vast,
In every glance, a shadow cast.
Moments held like pieces rare,
Life's rich canvas, emotionally bare.

In sepia tones, our laughter blooms,
Within the silence, love consumes.
Across the ages, stories blend,
In every heartbeat, we transcend.

Moments captured, forever bright,
We stand as one, a shared delight.
The world may change, but we remain,
In every joy, in every pain.

Woven into history's thread,
In dreams unheard, in words unsaid.
Each portrait tells a tale unique,
In whispered truths, it's love we seek.

From distant shores to worlds untold,
Through every season, we grow bold.
Together still, through ebb and flow,
In timeless echoes, our spirits glow.

Unraveling the Thread of Time

Ticking clocks and whispered fate,
Moments gathered, a fragile state.
Each second spins a tale to tell,
In every heartbeat, a magic spell.

Threads of gold and shadows blend,
In every loop, a journey penned.
We wander through this tapestry,
Drifting in sweet memory.

Time unravels; yet we hold tight,
As stars emerge to guide the night.
With every thread, connections weave,
In silken dreams, we dare believe.

Fragments scatter, yet love remains,
In every joy, in every pain.
We draw from threads that bind us tight,
In the darkest hour, we find the light.

Through ages past, we learn to see,
Every moment, a part of we.
With open hearts, we chase divine,
Together still, we thread through time.

Anchors in the Storm

Waves crash high against the shore,
Yet we stand firm, our spirits soar.
Tides may rise and tempests rage,
But love's embrace is our true cage.

Through darkest nights and fiercest gales,
Together we'll write our heart's tales.
Hand in hand, we brave the fray,
Anchored strong, come what may.

Stars may fade behind the cloud,
But in each other, we are proud.
Resilient souls, we stand as one,
In unity, we'll find the sun.

Let lightning strike and thunder roar,
We'll dance amidst the storm's uproar.
With every challenge, we will grow,
A bond that only we can know.

As winds may shift, our hearts align,
In every heartbeat, you are mine.
Through stormy skies, our path is clear,
Anchors of love, we persevere.

Where Hearts Converge

In whispers soft, our secrets bloom,
In shared laughter, we find room.
Paths entwined in life's great dance,
Every glance, a sweet romance.

Like rivers flow towards the sea,
Together, you and I will be.
With every step, hearts gently weave,
In this promise, we believe.

Embracing dreams, we dare to soar,
In each other's arms, we want more.
Time stands still, the world fades away,
In our haven, forever we'll stay.

Where shadows play and sunlight glows,
Our love, a garden, ever grows.
Through every storm, we'll find the way,
Where hearts converge, come what may.

Vibrations of Togetherness

In gentle hues, our spirits rise,
Echoing laughter fills the skies.
Every touch a melody sweet,
In harmony, our hearts will meet.

With every heartbeat, rhythms blend,
A symphony that will not end.
In every glance, a spark ignites,
Together we chase the brightest lights.

Through silent moments, connection deep,
A promise made, forever to keep.
With every word, a bridge we build,
In love's embrace, our souls are filled.

Across the miles, the music flows,
A dance of love, where time bestows.
In every note, we find our place,
Vibrations strong, in each embrace.

As twilight falls and stars appear,
In every heartbeat, you are near.
Together, we'll break every chain,
Vibrations of love, forever sustain.

The Palette of Connection

Colors blend on canvas wide,
With every stroke, our hearts collide.
Vibrant hues of joy and grace,
In this masterpiece, we find our space.

Each moment caught, a fleeting glance,
In the tapestry of our dance.
Brush of laughter, shade of tears,
In our art, we conquer fears.

Together creating a world anew,
With splashes bold and whispers true.
In every line, our stories told,
A tapestry of love to hold.

With each new dawn, fresh colors rise,
As the sun paints across the skies.
In love's embrace, our hearts collide,
The palette of connection, our guide.

Through shadows cast and light that gleams,
We fashion life from shared dreams.
In every shade, our spirits soar,
In the artwork of love, forever more.

Love Beyond the Horizon

In twilight's glow, we find our way,
Where dreams and wishes softly sway,
Above the clouds, our hearts ignite,
A promise whispered through the night.

Hand in hand, we chase the sun,
With every step, our souls are one,
The waves may crash, the winds may howl,
Yet in your eyes, I see my vow.

Across the sea, the stars align,
In every heartbeat, your love shines,
Beyond the view where shadows blend,
Our story writes without an end.

Through stormy skies, we learn to fly,
Together, love will never die,
With every dawn, a new embrace,
In every moment, find your space.

As seasons change and timelines shift,
Our hearts remain a timeless gift,
Beyond the horizon, side by side,
In endless love, we will abide.

Chains of Unseen Light

Invisible threads bind us tight,
In the darkest hours, we find our light,
A gentle pull, despite the storm,
In unseen chains, our hearts transform.

Through shadows deep, we blaze like fire,
A bond that fuels our hidden desire,
With every glance, the world fades away,
In silent whispers, we find our way.

Time will bend and space will sway,
Yet our connection will never fray,
A dance of souls in rhythm true,
In cosmic echoes, I am with you.

The weight of love, both fierce and kind,
In every moment, peace we find,
With chains of light, we rise above,
Bound forever by the threads of love.

As stars align in the velvet night,
We soar together, hearts in flight,
Unseen but felt, these chains will guide,
In every heartbeat, always by your side.

Together Through the Ages

Through time's embrace, we weave a tale,
With every heartbeat, we shall not fail,
In ancient echoes, our spirits roam,
Together through the ages, we find home.

From distant shores to mountains high,
In every breath, our dreams will fly,
With hands entwined, we face the night,
In endless journeys, hearts ignite.

The past may linger, shadows fade,
In love's embrace, our fears evade,
For every storm, we sail the seas,
Together, love, we find our ease.

With each sunrise, a brand new start,
In woven memories, peace imparts,
Through ages vast, we'll make our mark,
In every silence, hear love's spark.

So here we stand, both strong and free,
In unity, our destiny,
Through all the epochs, forever true,
Together always, just me and you.

Souls Intertwined in Silence

In quiet moments, our spirits meet,
A harmony where silence is sweet,
With every glance, a world unfolds,
In whispered dreams, our love beholds.

Amidst the noise, we find our calm,
In hidden spaces, love's gentle balm,
Soul to soul, we share the night,
In sacred stillness, hearts take flight.

Beyond the words, our essence flows,
In tender glances, pure love grows,
Unspoken truths in every sigh,
In silence deep, we learn to fly.

Through every trial, hand in hand,
In quiet strength, forever stand,
Our souls entwined in the softest glow,
In silence, love will always show.

And as the stars begin to gleam,
In the still of night, we dare to dream,
Together bound, in whispered grace,
Souls intertwined, our perfect place.